Moved Out

of

Our Comfort Zone

by

Phyllis Porter Dolislager

Copyright 2007, 2009, 2010, 2011, 2012, 2013, 2014, 2017, 2018, 2019

13th printing

by Phyllis Porter Dolislager

Moved Out Of Our Comfort Zone

Printed in the United States of America
Published by CreateSpace

ISBN-13: 978-1499279382
ISBN-10: 1499279388

All rights reserved. No part of this publication may be reproduced or transmitted in any form or by any means without written permission of the author.

Unless otherwise indicated, all Scripture quotations are taken from the **Holy Bible, New Living Translation**, copyright 1996. Used by permission of Tyndale House Publishers, Inc., Wheaton, Illinois 60189. All rights reserved.

To purchase other books by the author visit: amazon.com

Dedication

☧ ☧ ☧

Lois Ann Dolislager

9-10-42 to 1-17-07

Donna, Lois and Ron

We were privileged to be there

when she moved on to Heaven.

Be very careful never to forget

what you have seen the Lord do for you.

Do not let these things escape from

your mind as long as you live!

And be sure to pass them on . . . .

Deuteronomy 4:9

Introduction

We've Moved . . . Again

Three times in twelve months . . . is enough!

**We plan to stay put until we move
to assisted living.**

This headline from our 2006 Christmas letter said it all. Since move #2, we've struggled to remember our address and our phone number. When we tried to update an account like frequent flyer points, they'd ask for our previous address, and we had no idea if it was Boynton Beach, Palm Beach or West Palm Beach. And for awhile our mail was being forwarded from all three cities.

Now we are in Townsend, Tennessee, and as we look back, we can see God's hand on all of those moves. He used each one to bring us to this point, in His time, for His purpose.

When Ron was asked to take a new job with World Mission Centre, it was with 100% certainty that we said, "Yes."

This saga actually began in May of 2005.

I'll go anywhere as long as it's forward.

David Livingston

Boynton Beach, FL 33426

Wait for the Lord;

Be strong and let your heart take courage;

Yes, wait for the Lord.

The Lord is my strength and my shield;

My heart trusts in Him, and I am helped.

Psalm 27:14; 28:7a NASB

Boynton Beach, Florida 33426

The third week-end in **May 2005**, Ron and I returned from a week at our timeshare. Suddenly I realized that I, a polio survivor, was experiencing hardly any pain. What had happened? What was the difference? And then we realized—for one week we'd lived in a one-bedroom apartment, and I had done a lot less walking!!

I casually mentioned to Ron that maybe we needed to downsize sooner, rather than later. (Ron was 61 and not ready for retirement.) However, having just spent a Saturday in the hot, Florida sun doing yard work, he readily agreed. Also South America Mission, where Ron was the Director of Finance, was preparing to move out of state in a year's time. So we decided that we'd sell our house and rent for a year in anticipation of the mission's move.

In fact, quite out of character for us, we even started looking for rentals before our house sold. And I prayed, asking God for a place with a view of the water. I enjoy the sunrise, but I knew that living on the ocean would definitely be out of the question financially. So I started reading ads for an apartment on the west side of the Intracoastal Waterway, which is also the less expensive side. That would include the view of the sunrise too.

We only went to see two properties. The first one was great, but the timing was a little ahead of the sale of our house. When I called later, they were converting to condos. The second property had so much land and so many boat slips between the small balcony and the water, that it was a BIG stretch of the imagination to call it water-front or even water-view. We passed on that one.

I returned to my search on the Internet. A property turned up. We went to check it out, even though it was on "the other side" of the Intracoastal. The apartment we were shown was in the middle of the building, with a great view of the parking lot and the adjacent property. The water view could only be seen from the balcony. I said that I was disappointed with the view.

What we heard next was magic—or was it God? The property manager had a corner apartment, right on the water, that she hadn't shown anyone. To make a long story short, that's where we ended up. I truly believe that God had kept it, just waiting for us to show up.

When people came to visit us or just asked where we were living, everyone was amazed that we lived in Palm Beach, right on the Intracoastal. Our front balcony was only about 15 feet from the water's edge. It was amazing, AND it provided us with the window of opportunity to say that our apartment was an answer to prayer.

It's a marvelous story of Him giving us the desires of our hearts, and the water view provided the inspiring back-drop for the writing of my latest book, *Simple Ways to Share Your Faith.*

We put our 2,000 sq. ft. house on the market and sold it for full price the end of July. We were ready to close the middle of September, but the deal fell through because of undisclosed contingencies on our buyer's house. We canceled our 40th anniversary trip to the Grand Canyon and Sedona, put the house back on the market, added $10,000 to the price, and sold it in two days. Then that sale fell through over the security deposit. But there were our original buyers waiting with another full-price offer, plus more.

We gave away most of our furniture. The dining room set, the kitchen furniture, and the TV, all went to a missionary family home from Argentina less than a year. Family members took a lot, especially the family heirlooms like my Grandma De Boer's marble top chest. We invited two young neighbor families in to help themselves to Ron's tools. Everything in the garage went. By year's end, we'd even given away both weeks of our timeshare.

Three Gatekeepers

1. Is it kind?

2. Is it necessary?

3. Is it true?

Arab Proverb

Palm Beach, FL 33480

The voice of the Lord is upon the waters;

The God of glory thunders.

The Lord is over many waters.

Psalm 29:3 NASB

(This scripture was from my first devotional time in our Palm Beach apartment.)

Palm Beach, Florida 33480

September 1st we moved into the 1150 sq. ft. rental apartment in Palm Beach. The youth group from West Pines Baptist Church moved us along with the help of some friends. Cheryl Arflin directed everyone with placement of furniture and boxes as they were brought in. Jan Wright helped me settle the kitchen. Their husbands helped Ron with various tasks.

We sent out a standard e-mail announcement with a generic moving-type graphic. When our friends heard exactly what our new address was, and that it was Palm Beach, their many responses required another email. Here it is:

It now appears that we're on the verge of committing one of the biggest faux pas of all time for a missionary: moving to a Palm Beach address. Your collective responses to our email announcement have been "interesting." In fact, I'm beginning to think that maybe my mother was right to worry about "what will people think?" And Ron, who's always concerned with his support level at South America Mission/SAM, is ready to get us a P.O. Box in Podunk.

But in the midst of all the good-natured comments, which I'm hoping was your way of having some fun, we got a laugh or two. AND would you believe, one friend, Ken, even offered to help us move. Of course, he also wanted to "use our private beach!"

First of all, we're not buying—we're renting . . . a 2 bedroom/2 bath, 1150 sq. ft condo. It does have a view of the Intracoastal Waterway, which we're excited about. It even has a balcony from which to view the water. And . . . across the street, A1A, we have access to a private beach. (Now how in the world did Ken know about that??)

Secondly, that was NOT a photo of our new, or of our old, place. It's a stock photo. I don't know if you all were just trying to be nice, or what, but I can't believe how many of you were impressed with our "gorgeous place," "Palm Beach….Wow!!! Cool, Dudes." "Ocean Blvd., Palm Beach sounds very exclusive! Are you nearer to Rush Limbaugh or Donald Trump?"(The answer was Donald Trump.) And then there was, "Wow—I am so impressed with how professional everything looks."

Believe me, our current place looks like a jig saw puzzle that's been thrown around. The new place is bare and white. So sorry to disappoint you all! Perhaps our son Fred, who was here last week-end, got it right with his comments, "Whose house is that? Whose stuff is in there?" Another friend complimented us on our "box furniture."

One friend, who is also contemplating a move, said, "It all looks so organized! I'm jealous." (Now she knows our secret: fake photo.) And another honest soul, "I'm jealous. What a great new neighborhood." Followed by wonder and amazement, "I can't believe you're going to be an Islander! I hope you'll still e-mail us little people!" (We will!)

Why don't you come for a visit and enjoy the blessing that we truly believe is from God? We'll have a hide-a-bed in the office (second bedroom) and a futon in the living room. We've sold our house and will be paying our rent with the interest that the money will be earning. (We could read your minds wondering, how in the world those missionaries are able to do that?)

SAM is studying a relocation of its U.S. office. Hopefully in a year there will be a decision, and then we'll know what our next move will be. If they decide to stay put, we hope that the prices will have leveled out or the real estate bubble will have burst. If not, we'll rent another year. God is in control. And you all, dear friends and relatives, are an indication that He not only cares for us, but that He truly has a sense of humor too.

Thanks for caring enough to . . . not let our change of address go unnoticed!

October 21, 2005, the Friday before Hurricane Wilma hit, we signed all the papers to sell the house. The new owners walked through and also signed all the papers, but no money changed hands. (When there's a named storm off the coast of Florida, banks will not wire money.) Then the hurricane came, and we had no idea who owed the house. Ron put the storm shutters up. We hunkered down in our apartment. (Wilma started on the west coast as a category one. We expected it to be just a tropical storm when it got to us, but it strengthened and became a category three. Wilma was the fourth costliest hurricane to hit the U.S. with damages totaling $11.4 billion.)

During "the eye" of Hurricane Wilma, we received a call from a former neighbor. He said that the roof had come off our sun porch and landed on the neighbor's car. Wow! When the hurricane passed, we received another call saying that it wasn't our roof, but someone else's. Our house survived unharmed, even though there was a lot of damage in the neighborhood. Thank you, Lord.

We had such an unusual experience during Hurricane Wilma in 2005 that it's a story that grabs people's attention, and in the process they hear how God showed Ron that it was time to leave a job he'd had for 24 years.

A few weeks earlier, Ron and I had decided to take two weeks of our vacation and visit Tennessee and northern Florida to check out the retirement possibilities as normal retirement was about five years away. This also meant checking out the job market. (Living on just Social Security didn't seem feasible, and there wouldn't be a pension from SAM.) With that in mind, Ron had gotten out his resume, updated it, and had a friend give it a facelift by reformatting it.

But before Ron had a chance to print it out, Hurricane Wilma struck. After five days without power, we decided to accept some friends' offer of hospitality. Of course, Ron took the laptop computer along and the back-up disc from his computer.

While there, he remembered that he'd never printed out his reformatted resume. So Ron emailed it (across the room) to our friend. Our friend proceeded to open the file, print it, and then he read it.

What he did next still amazes us. He emailed it, without asking, to someone who had been looking to hire a controller. Ron's experience as a Finance Director in the non-profit world was not only nicely detailed, but nicely formatted as well. Two days later Ron received a phone call asking him to come in for an interview at a large, downtown church.

After some negotiations, he accepted the new position at First Baptist Church of West Palm Beach. Ron had been at South America Mission for 24 years. This job was not something he had sought out. But when God speaks so clearly (Or was it a push?), gives His directions, we've both learned to listen.

Ron resigned from South America Mission on his 24th anniversary, December 1. (It was seven months since we'd gone to the timeshare.) January 1, he started as Controller at First Baptist of West Palm Beach overseeing an $8 million budget. AND would you believe it—the apartment with a water view was closer to the new job than to the old one!

Once again we were assured that when we spend time alone with God, He speaks. He leads. He points. He directs. And sometimes He pushes.

We continued to enjoy life in Palm Beach, and with it came many opportunities to share our faith with residents of our building. We met and made friends with interesting and special people. Paul and Lydia from Montreal were our closest friends. They taught us the ways of the French including the greeting kiss on both cheeks and the pleasure of a home-made, epicurean dinner with several courses that we enjoyed for about three hours.

And of course, we delighted in being so close to Lake Worth Beach and the restaurants, not to mention our own private beach on the ocean, just across the street. And through an unnamed contact, we even enjoyed lunch at Mar-A-Lago, Donald Trump's home and private club.

We had a lot of company! Almost every Saturday we ate breakfast at the beach with friends. My mother spent a week with us. That year both brothers and my sister and their spouses visited us.

We thoroughly enjoyed sharing our blessing of living on the Intracoastal Waterway. We could even see the water from our bed. We ate breakfast almost every morning on our balcony, and we were always looking to see the fish jump. And the sailboats and yachts that passed by were spectacular.

Once we saw a large tree float by on a barge. The next day we read in The Shiny Sheet (Palm Beach's newspaper) that it was a 60-foot tall and 50-foot wide kapok tree. It had traveled by water from Fort Lauderdale over the week-end. "The Florida Department of Transportation had authorized $140,000 to buy, relocate, plant, irrigate and insure the tree for one year, town officials said." (A little sample of life in Palm Beach.)

But maybe the best . . . was the sunset over the water. We never tired of watching it and enjoying it. Another spectacular was viewing fireworks over the water. Fourth of July we saw them set off from three different cities. And New Year's Eve, we viewed Donald Trump's amazing fireworks show.

My mother was right: living in Palm Beach was like one continuous vacation. We couldn't fuss about having had to cancel our 40th anniversary trip.

In early spring of 2006, I found out about the East Tennessee Mountain Writers Conference in Oak Ridge, Tennessee. It was near Fred's house—I could attend, deduct the cost as a business expense, and then visit Fred's family. Little did I know that God had another reason for my attendance.

In a workshop I met Ina Painter, a local realtor. And a few days later I found out the important part that she was going to play in our future.

Townsend, TN 37882

The Purchase

Whatever decisions you face today,

commit them to God and

ask Him to guide you—and He will.

--Billy Graham

Townsend, TN 37882

The Purchase

It was one of those first's in my life. Our older son (wise age of 39) sat me (wise age of 60ish) down and asked me just how much thought had gone into my desire to leave an apartment in sunny South Florida and buy a log cabin in the Smoky Mountains. Of course, he and I both knew the answer to that: None . . . Zero . . . Zip.

Until that beautiful April day, enhanced by the spring blooms of Tennessee's dogwood and redbuds, I had envisioned Ron and me retiring in a condo with little maintance. That was before our daughter-in-law and I had toured some overpriced, under-designed condos on a lake and a golf course.

The following day Fred and I visited some condo complexes in the city of Knoxville. They may have been more in our price range, but not one of them held any promise for a wheelchair user. All our hopes seemed to have gone askew until I started looking through a local real estate magazine which Sue had picked up, and my eye zeroed in on a log cabin with the caption, "Handicap Accessible."

Fred and I, and our realtor, Ina Painter, then headed

east to Townsend, one of the entrances to the Great Smoky Mountain National Park. After following a winding road, up and down and around, we saw it: a perfect, 1200 sq. ft., 2 bedroom, 2 bath, log cabin in the mountains . . . without any steps!

After I'd been inside about two minutes, had inhaled the knotty pine fragrance and checked out the fireplace, I announced, "We'll take it." Of course, neither Ina nor Fred paid any attention to me; they continued looking around, so I followed them.

Fred took lots of photos with his digital camera for Ron. I finally came to my senses and decided that I wasn't going to buy our retirement place without Ron. (Give me some credit, Fred.) But to my defense, Ron fell in love with the log cabin just from the photos.

Two weeks later Ron and I returned, looked at a couple of other cabins for price comparison, and made our offer. (Of course, all the others had steps and none of them were brand new like ours.) The builder, Matt Kobolak, had purposely built the cabin to be accessible. He was thinking ahead to the boomer population getting ready for retirement and that very few cabins on the local rental programs were handicap accessible.

The cabin has wide, 36" doorways, a Jacuzzi tub and a free-standing shower in each bathroom. The closets are walk-in or roll-in. The clothes rods could be put at any height. Even the door to the back deck is 36" wide and accommodating, and the doors all have lever handles instead of knobs. The only thing missing in our cabin was the use of rocker switches instead of typical light switches. More and more builders around the country are using Universal Design as they build.

Retirement or handicap living can be in the mountains and near natural attractions. Townsend even has a special handicap picnic area along the Little River. And just yesterday I realized that unlike South Florida, I can usually find a Handicap Parking space, and the electric cart in Target was almost brand new. It ran perfectly. The Smoky Mountain National Park even has an Accessibility Guide.

We are 18 miles from a major airport, 16 miles from Maryville that has all the medical care and shopping that we could want or need, and 17 miles from Pigeon Forge with its tourist attractions. Yet we have "the peaceful side of the mountains" in Townsend, including craftsmen, artists, the Heritage Center, food, music and recreation. (I need to get a job working for the Chamber of Commerce!)

Selling our 2,000 sq. ft. house and moving to an 1150 sq. ft. condo in 2005 was our transition into downsizing and soon to be retirement living. Fewer steps immediately made a difference for me with my post-polio. I had been using my power chair almost full-time in our larger home. Now when post-polio causes my leg to give out, I am able to easily use my power chair.

Thank goodness, "Handicap Accessible" is becoming more and more available. Don't limit yourself. Be aware. Look for a builder and/or a realtor who will listen to and accommodate your needs. The options are out there, but it's up to us to discover them.

When your children or your friends sit you down for a little talk about your desire for something different for your housing choices, tell them about Ron and me. We love it. We're glad that we didn't settle for the ordinary or usual. However we did settle only an hour away from Fred & Sue and their kids. Grandchildren Gerrit & Carolina have already claimed the loft in our log cabin as their territory!

Article published in New Mobility Magazine, May 2007

West Palm Beach, FL 33417

Your love for one another will prove to the world

that you are my disciples.

John 13:35

West Palm Beach, FL 33417

With Ron working at First Baptist Church of West Palm Beach, we knew that we wouldn't be heading out of state with South American Mission and that we needed to find cheaper housing. A friend in our Sunday school class told us of an apartment that she had for rent in West Palm Beach. We agreed to rent it even before we looked at it. The moving date was set for July 8.

Because it'd only been ten months since our friends had helped us move from Boynton Beach to Palm Beach, this time we hired a moving company to do the heavy lifting.

As we down-sized again, from our Palm Beach condo to our West Palm Beach apartment, we gave away more things. Again God sent our two angels, Ron & Cheryl Arflin, who helped us put things in place, and they even hung pictures on the walls in our new apartment. Another blessing, neighbors from 25 years ago, Ed & Jan Wright, were neighbors at our WPB address.

We closed on our log cabin home on July 6. Actually, Fred closed for us. We went to the Rooms To Go store in West Palm Beach and picked out some furniture, which Fred ordered for us in Knoxville. Sue bought the basics that we'd need to set up housekeeping, and she and/or Fred were on site when the furniture was delivered. Sue also organized the cupboards and had the cabin livable for us.

A few years ago my doctor had told me that one of the best things that I could do for my health was to get out of the heat and humidity of August and September in south Florida. Now that we owned a place, the decision was made that I'd go there for those two months. With that short term goal in mind, Ron and I set out for Tennessee on July 21. I had lived in the West Palm Beach apartment for only two weeks.

Our third day in Tennessee, Gerrit & Carolina stayed overnight. We were ready to stay full-time right then. We loved being close to grandchildren.

The 27th of July, our angel, Cheryl Arflin, once again helped us settle in. She flew up and took us shopping for a couch, a sofa bed and chairs. Then she went back into town for rugs, accessories, etc. This continued until Sunday the 30th, when she and Ron flew back to Florida. (This year we celebrated our anniversary, with Cheryl, over a four-course fondue dinner at a local bed and breakfast.

I appreciate what I can do and those who God sends to help me. This continues to amaze me. Fred, Sue, and Cheryl Arflin. What would I have done without them? Only a few years ago I wouldn't have needed their help—I was one self-sufficient person. But now I have to trust God more to provide what I need, and surely this isn't bad!

Journal 7/31, 2006

Is my will in harmony with God's? Is my desire to live in just one location (Tennessee) wrong? Would God give us this place, but leave Ron's job in West Palm Beach? Will I accept His will, no matter what? Open my eyes and my heart, Dear God, to know and to do your will.

Journal 8/7/2006

Visit from the Bear

At three PM this Friday, I was outdoors at the roadside helping our newspaper delivery man attach a tube for the newspaper to our mailbox post. He said, "Don't say a word, but there's a bear walking to your porch." I looked up, and sure enough a LARGE bear was walking up to the porch. Then he walked around in front of the porch, down the bank on the other side and into the neighbor's driveway. He continued walking down to the turn-around at the end of the road and then into the woods.

The newspaper man said that he'd never been that close to a bear w/o being in his truck. We must have been only 10 feet away from him. I think I was numb. When the bear got beyond our neighbor's, I said, "Shall I get the camera?"

He said, "No." We just stood there, quite still, and didn't move.

Earlier he had confirmed that the tracks on the side of the bank were bear tracks. When the bear returned this afternoon, he came up from the north side of the house. The man said that the bear was marking his territory and that he'd be back, and that I should be very careful.

Evidently the rainfall has been low, and the bears are looking for food. I thought they only came out at dawn and twilight, but I WAS WRONG.

Enough excitement for today, I hope . . . .

Journal 8/18/2006

Mother and Darcia came and spent five days with me. Almost every day we all talked to Ron. They continued to encourage him to take early retirement at the end of the year, 12/31/06. That way he would have been in the job at First Baptist for a full year. They also added their decorative touch to our cabin and filled it with lots of black bears!

August 21st Ron turned in his Letter of Retirement. They thanked him for giving them so much advance notice. Later in the week, the new senior pastor resigned because false statements were discovered on his resume as well as improprieties in his personal finances. When it was all said and done, the whole experience cost the church about $200,000 for moving, severance, etc. and he (the new senior pastor) had been on staff less than a month.

September 18, the Executive Pastor, Kevin Mahoney, asked Ron if he'd take his retirement September 30 because the church was struggling with its finances. This threw us for a loop as we'd been planning for December 31.

God's in control, and we can see some positives in it too. There are many details to trust God for, but nothing that He can't handle. I pray that we will discern His will in everything.

Journal 9/19/20006

Ron went to work this AM. At noon he returned to the apartment, loaded up the car, and headed for Tennessee: The first step on our complete relocation. God's in control.

Journal 9/20/2006

September 25, we took Fred's pick-up and headed back to Florida. Ron went to work the 27th and I started packing. He worked the 28th and 29th. We said our good-bye's to his staff, to our Sunday school class, and on Oct. 2 to special friends. The Wrights helped us load a U-haul trailer the morning of October 3rd. Ed gave Ron some trailer towing lessons, and we were on our way before noon.

We felt so badly about leaving the rental apartment after only three months (I had lived there a total of three weeks.) that we left it completely furnished, right down to the dishes and pots and pans. We took our computers, office materials, clothes and some smaller items. Then we were off to our new log cabin home and life in Tennessee.

Townsend, TN 37882

The Permanent Move

It is not that we think we can do anything

of lasting value by ourselves.

Our only power and success come from God.

II Corinthians 3:5

Townsend, TN 37882

The Permanent Move

We experienced in thirteen months what some people never experience in thirteen years. And at the same time God gave us many opportunities to share and minister along the way. Truly we were blessed.

Getting unpacked seemed to be just the beginning. I don't know if it was because of the suddenness of the change or just the change itself, but life was unsettled for a long while. We had a lot of decisions to make and a new routine to follow. A lot of nights I didn't sleep well.

Should Ron look for a job or should we try to live on social security for a year while we unwound? And everyone seemed to have an opinion that they freely shared with us. They varied from actually finding a job for Ron, which he ended up declining, to telling him to enjoy retirement, to telling him that age 62 was just too young to stop working!

Ordinary things like getting new car tags and driver's licenses ended up taking five trips into town. Then just as soon as that was finally worked out, we decided that we really didn't need two cars anymore. Finding a grocery store that carried products that we liked and a health food store that carried Ginger Brew were also two big things for us. And where would we get our hair cut?

I also needed to find a doctor right away as a signature was required for a handicap permit for the car, and I also wanted a flu shot. Through searching the Internet, I found a medical group in town, and we're very happy with them. The doctor that we were assigned even graduated from the University of Florida. We joke that he's "twelve years old." But for a patient with a chronic illness, he's superb.

During this time I had a lot of work: two manuscripts to edit, two grant proposals to write, and a fund-raising letter to write. So I put Ron to work, and he didn't even have the pressure of leaving home. Yard work was different too. Ron was concerned about what to do with all the leaves and pine needles that fell.

But there were wonderful things that happened too! We got to help Carolina celebrate her birthday. We enjoyed Thanksgiving at Fred's house. (He had shot a wild turkey.) Ron put out a bird feeder. Gerrit and Carolina came to spend the night frequently. We got to enjoy the fall colors—it'd been 25 years! We were able to drive to Arkansas for lunch with

Tom. We saw Gerrit graduate from Cub Scouts to Boy Scouts. We saw snow. A black bear came by our front porch—twice that we witnessed first-hand!

And friends still come to visit. Now they're usually on their way to Florida or to Pigeon Forge.

Church of the Cove was different from what we'd been used to, but we loved it! Our praise team had some of the best guitar pickers. The dress for everyone was casual—jeans and tennis shoes were just fine. Potluck dinners were phenomenal!

At one they had a cake auction, and all the cakes were made by the men. They each told a little story about their recipe or method, and one even did some fancy steppin'. Prices went up to $100 per cake too—all for the building fund.

Then there are the sermons. We never fail to get some take-away message, and the Southern expressions put a smile on our face.

We loved life in Townsend in our little log cabin. We almost seemed to be settling in. We were meeting neighbors through a small group from church—The Mustard Seeds. Life was good.

Expanding our comfort zone

is expanding our possibilities.

It's living with passion, not drama,

finding balance and wholeness.

Happiness is a journey, not a destination.

Gary Laundre

Ron's Sister Lois Ann

Set your sights on the realities of heaven,

Let heaven fill your thoughts.

Colossians 3:1b; 2a

A Sudden Trip to Detroit

We had known for a couple of weeks that Ron's sister, Lois, was not well. She had been in the hospital and then rehabilitation with breathing difficulties. We were kept abreast of her progress by six women from her church who had surrounded her with care, assistance, and their friendship. (Ron called them the Magnificent Six: Gail Elenbaas, Jenni Dunn, Char Gelderloos, Elizabeth Bowersox, Gloria Jongsma, Vicki Hoolsema.)

Lots of phone calls and emails kept us connected. But on January 8, everyone was in agreement that it was time for us to go to Detroit. We spent the 9th packing and making preparation to be gone for awhile.

Please God may we show Lois Your love and help her to accept and plan for the future.

Journal 1/9/2007

"Much of our lives is flying (as in trapeze) . . . . Let's trust the Great Catcher."

Henri J. M. Nouwen
Bread for the Journey

We got to Detroit and checked into our room at 6 PM and 10 minutes later got a call that Lois had arrested. (Her heart stopped.) We gathered our things and headed to the hospital. Lois had asked for no heroics, but through a mix-up with her health directive, we found her on a ventilator.

Ron and I said the 23rd Psalm to her, and I read some songs and sang some to her. We also showed her photos of Fred's and Tom's families and of our log cabin.

The next day Ron and I and three of Lois's friends met with the End of Life staff. What to do? God's in control.

Journal 1/11/2007

"Let's not be afraid to look at everything that has brought us to where we are now and trust that we will soon see in it the guiding hand of a loving God."
Nouwen

"Prayer is the bridge between our conscious and unconscious lives….To pray is to connect these two sides of our lives by going to the place where God dwells." Nouwen

Ron and Donna met with the End-of-Life Staff today. Times are hectic and emotional.

Journal 1/15/2007

I don't know what today will bring. There is so much to do. Thank goodness Donna is here as I'm about to collapse. I even had Ron bring my power chair into the hotel. I can't begin to think about walking to the restaurant today. Last night the pain never really went away.

Ron & Donna were gone all day working on Lois's affairs.

Journal 1/16/2007

"We are unique human beings, each with a call to realize in life."

Nouwen

Ron & Donna had a meeting with the End of Life staff again today. Lois's pastor visited, and she told him that she was ready to go. Once the breathing tube was removed, she only lived ten minutes. We stood around her body crying and commenting that she was now walking in heaven—with a straight spine. It was 4:50 PM.

Journal 1/17/2007

Lois's Handicap Accessible Van

What is faith? It is the confident assurance

that what we hope for is going to happen.

It is the evidence of things we cannot yet see.

Hebrews 11:1

Miracles Are Handicap Accessible

When I first met Howard Mades, he was walking with two strange-looking canes. Noticing my puzzled look, he proudly explained that they were polo mallets turned upside down. So in addition to meeting one of the members of the post-polio support group, I also met a polo aficionado.

I soon found out that there was a lot more to Howard than polio and polo. As we exercised together in the warm water pool at the Rehab Center, I grew to appreciate his sense of humor, his keen intellect on almost any subject, and his analysis of polio: *the gift that keeps on giving.*

Little by little our friendship grew. When we moved to Boynton Beach, we were almost neighbors. And when Howard broke his leg, we took him groceries, etc. We were also kept abreast of the Canadian friend he met playing bridge on the Internet. Wow! One thing led to another, and we were invited to Howard and Jane's wedding.

Our friendship has continued—often providing one another a listening ear. It's been interesting how our down-hill slide with post-polio syndrome has mirrored each other—even though Howard is a few steps (no pun intended) ahead of me in the descent.

But sure enough, if I was having a bad week, he would be too. Sometimes in Jane's concern for Howard, she'd call me and ask if I'd ever experienced x, y, or z. Fortunately our friendship continued even with us living in Tennessee.

Sometime in the fall of '06, I received a call from Jane telling me of Howard's latest crisis. He was unable to transfer from his car to his wheelchair. In desperation, a friend had lifted him out. As you can imagine, this was a traumatic event for Howard, and his response of sleeping several hours following that frightened Jane.

A week or two later, Howard called and told me about the same incident. I listened and commiserated. I also suggested that it might be time for a wheelchair accessible van. He immediately countered that no way did he have $30 or $40 thousand. But perhaps the seed was planted.

January 10, 2007, Ron and I headed to Detroit to help his sister Lois, also a polio survivor, find an apartment or assisted living place. Ten minutes after we got to our hotel, we were summoned to the hospital as she had arrested. Due to a mix-up in her health directive, they had revived her and put her on a respirator.

(We learned from this experience to have medical directives in writing, to have a current will, and to have in writing what you want for a funeral/memorial service and burial.) Lois passed away a week later.

Lois came down with polio when she was seven and lived the rest of her life in a wheelchair. She went to Wayne State University in Detroit—it was one of the first to be handicap accessible. She became a social worker for the state of Michigan. Upon retirement, she taught American Girls, volunteered in an Arab-American Friendship Center teaching English to the women, and she was active in her church. Lois's friends drove her to most of these functions in her handicap accessible van.

Ron was named executor of her will, and the van was part of the estate. One of many questions before him was what to do with it. We live in Tennessee, but the van was in Detroit . . . where we hardly knew a soul.

Then the miraculous started to unfold. Howard's name popped into my mind. I called him. Yes, he was interested. (The van only had 40,000 miles and would be significantly less money than a new one.) But—it was in Lois's name, and it was in Michigan, and Howard was in Florida.

My brother Ron lived 3 ½ hours away and "just happened" to be coming to Detroit. He was bringing his sons to the Auto Show. So my Ron, using his POA, signed the title off. Bryan, my nephew, drove the van north to my brother's home where Ron proceeded to do the title work.

Wait—it gets better! My brother and his wife had a trip to Florida already planned . . . and on February 10, they delivered the van to Howard! By this time Howard was actually looking forward to the van as he'd experienced another "no-go" with his leg function.

We think that Lois would be pleased to know that her van was used by another polio survivor. Ron and I and my brother are thrilled to be facilitators of this small miracle.

**Article written for post-polio newsletter: The Sunshine Special, March 2007

We never test the resources of God

until we attempt the impossible.

F. B. Meyer

"Get Out of the Boat"

*A chance of a lifetime . . . and the eleven disciples
who stayed in the boat missed it . . .
a chance to walk by faith.*

Ron's newsletter

Dolislager Drum

March 2007

Phyllis and I have lived in Townsend, TN, for six months now. Our heads have almost stopped spinning from the four moves and the job changes we experienced. Retirement still feels like work. Good friends, Tom & Betty Combs, stopped by on their way to Florida this January. Being wise and full of years, they declared that I really was too young to retire.

* * *

A couple of weeks later, Willie and Lydia Crew called to see if we would be home February 15. We thought it was just a social call. For six years Phyllis has done grant writing and other work for their organization, World Mission Centre—a mission agency from South Africa with a U.S. office in South Carolina. Willie is the founder and International Director: a business man turned pastor/missionary. We were impressed by the mission and what the Holy Spirit has led them to accomplish.

Their visit turned out to be another opportunity to walk by faith—another chance to move out of our comfort zone. The Crews' trip, from Columbia, SC to our home, was to ask me (Ron) if I would be the Finance Director of their new and expanding Live School ministry.

I knew immediately that my answer was, "Yes." In fact, I had often thought that I would like to be a part of what God is doing through World Mission Centre and Live School. We are honored and pleased to share in this ministry. And we do not have to move again, thanks to our high speed Internet connection.

The vision of **Live School** is to train thousands of people who live in places where they have no access to formal training to be missionaries.

> **Live School is a cutting-edge tool prepared to train a world-wide mission force.**

For I know the plans I have for you,

declares the Lord,

plans to give you hope and a future.

Jeremiah 29:10

2010 Update

Lantana, FL 33462

The Purchase

Lantana, FL 33462

The Purchase

We spent our first winter in Tennessee. It was a mild winter, and we enjoyed being near family and our new friends in Townsend. But when the fall of 2007 came, it was cold. I told Ron that he'd better take me back to FL for the winter.

I'd always heard about people with post-polio having a problem with the cold. But I'd lived in south FL for 25 years and hadn't experienced it myself. But I soon learned.

Through a friend we heard about a unit to rent in Palm Beach, right across A1A where we had rented before. This time we were on the ocean!

The next winter, 2008, we returned again. But paying rent wasn't much to Ron's liking. The housing market had hit bottom, Ron thought maybe we should look to buy. We remembered back in 2003, when looking for a car, we had responded to an ad in the newspaper.

That took us to a 55+ community which impressed us. It was secluded, but just off the main roads. We wondered if we could find it after five years. And after a few wrong turns, we did! We drove around the community writing down the phone numbers of units that were for sale.

We went to our friend Sherwin Harris, a realtor who lived in our building in Palm Beach. He made the contacts, and we went looking at the various condos. To make a long story short, we bought an 1150 sq. ft condo in Pointe Overlook in Lantana for $25,000 on January 23, 2009.

Through a contact at our Bible study class at First Baptist WPB, we were introduced to Brad Mousel. He worked his magic on the unit, and we moved in on March 1.

Now we're enjoying the best of two worlds. Our permanent address is still Tennessee. But when it gets cold, we head to Florida for a few months.

Faith-takers get out of their comfort zones.

God is always on the move.

If we become comfortable,

we may not be moving with God.

2014 Final Note

Yes, we were moved out of our comfort zone, but we wouldn't change a thing. God has been beside us for this entire journey.

The fact that you're holding this book in your hand means that you might have experienced one of the times when God gave me a push, and I offered you this book.

The book is now in its 12th printing, and I give away about 100 copies a year.

2016 Update

We sold our log cabin home in June of 2016 and are once again permanent Florida residents living in our condo. (We couldn't afford two properties.) God's plan continues to unfold in our lives. We look forward to what the future brings.

2017 Update

Our Return Move to TN

One God-encounter can radically change the direction of your life forever.
Robin Betram
No Regrets

Condo in Lenoir City, TN

July 17 ~ A new friend, Bonnie Hodges Leech, was looking at two condos in our community of Pointe Overlook in Lantana, FL. It happened that I knew both potential sellers, and so I accompanied her. Bonnie had looked at four or five other units, and as we went through those two, it became apparent to me what she was looking for.

That evening our son Fred called from TN saying that he had found a place for us in TN. He was going to go look at it that week-end. This was a completely new idea for us. We thought that we were in FL for the rest of our lives.

During dinner, I said to Ron, "Bonnie wants to buy a condo just like ours. What do you think? Is it time for us to sell?"

He said, "Yes."
I sent Bonnie this text message at 7:14 pm:

Buy our condo? We've always known that we'd end up in TN sometime, and we just spoke with our son. He told us of some options. So, we're wondering if you would be interested.

Bonnie replied:
What? You might move? My head is spinning! Yes, of course I would love to have a chance to own your beautiful home. I am still in shock though.

So are we. Feel free to call and/or come over tonight or tomorrow. You are the only one who we're telling at this time.

What time will you be up, lol!!! Tomorrow morning would be great. Just name the time.

We'll be done with breakfast at 8:30.

I'll be there at 8:31, promptly.

If this works, it truly will be a God-thing!

Amazing occurrences have taken place this month and just this past week-end especially. No pressure and no expectations on my part. I hope I can sleep.

July 18 ~ Bonnie came over, and we gave her the complete tour of our condo. (She had been there several times before.) She wanted to buy it. We agreed on a price.

Next question: how do we handle the buy/sell paperwork? Bonnie's friend gave her the blank buy/sell forms, and Ron filled them out. Then he had our realtor friend in TN, Ina Painter, review them. He contacted the title company where we had originally closed on the condo eight years earlier.

July 20 ~ At the Title Company the paperwork was signed and earnest money deposited.

July 22 ~ We left for TN to hopefully find a condo near Fred and Sue.

July 24 ~ We looked at condos with our realtor and daughter-in-law, Sue. About noon we decided to return to the first one, asked Fred to join us, and we all thought that was THE one. Went to Aubry's for lunch, joined by granddaughter Carolina, wrote out a proposal. It was accepted an hour later.

July 25 ~ Sister, Darcia Kelley came from Michigan to help us in our house hunt. As we'd already bought one the day before, we enjoyed our time together with everyone playing Wizard and going ziplining in the Smokies. (Darcia returned the first week-end in September, joining Fred and Sue as they helped us unpack and get settled.)

July 28 ~ We left to return to Florida.

August 27 ~ Fred flew into Ft. Lauderdale to drive our loaded U-Haul to TN.

August 28 ~ We closed on our FL condo at 10 AM in FL, and hit the road for Tennessee.

August 29 ~ We had a walk-thru at our new condo in TN at 3pm.

August 30 ~ We closed on our condo in TN at 4 pm.

August 31 ~ Hurricane Irma was getting everyone's attention. People asked us how we escaped Hurricane Irma, and we could only respond that it was God's timing . . . something that we hadn't planned or anticipated.

Hurricane Irma—One for the Record Books

Hurricane Irma, was upgraded to a Category 3 storm and likely to become a high-end Category 4 or 5. Irma was forecast to begin affecting the Leeward Islands on Tuesday, with Puerto Rico, the Bahamas, and possibly the mainland U.S.[1]

~ ~ ~

If Irma had made her appearance three days earlier, we wouldn't have been able to complete our closing in Florida. FL banks have this ruling that they won't wire/transfer money when there's a named storm at sea!

We know this to be a fact. When we were selling our house in Boynton Beach in 2005, Hurricane Wilma made her appearance. Even though all the paperwork was completed and had been signed. we didn't get our money for over two weeks.

~ ~ ~

Today: September 2017 ~ We still respond that it was God's timing—something that we hadn't planned or anticipated.

Update: November 2017 ~ We just heard that the damage caused by Hurricane Irma, added to previous problems from Hurricane Wilma, to the properties of Pointe Overlook, especially the roofs, will cost the community $1.2 million. This will amount to about $7500 for each owner of a one-bedroom condo like ours. God surely did spare us.

"There are times in life when the very best thing we can do is to 'sit still' . . . and let the Redeemer redeem. God doesn't need my help to redeem my situation."

--Jack Hayford
A New Time & Place

Without Me you can do nothing.   John 15:5

[1]Irma was classified as a Category 5 hurricane for three consecutive days, longer than any other Atlantic hurricane. Karen Clark and Co., a Boston-based firm that analyzes risk, estimated total losses, including the Caribbean, at $25 billion. Florida accounts for most of the $18 billion in the U.S., followed by Georgia, South Carolina and Alabama. The estimate covers damage to buildings and their contents, other insured structures, and vehicles and the disruption to business. It does not include crop losses or losses covered by the nation's flood insurance program, Clark said.

Is God speaking to you right now?

Tell Him you're listening.

He leads. He points. He directs.

And sometimes He pushes.

He's there 24/7.

Don't be afraid, for I am with you.

Don't be discouraged, for I am your God.

I will strengthen you and help you.

I will hold you up with my victorious right hand.

Isaiah 41:10

Made in United States
Cleveland, OH
24 January 2025